To Uncle Jim, my brother ~Chris

James to Jude

A Lyrical Paraphrase

Grace, Peace, & Eternal Life to you & ALL your loved ones from God our Father & from our Creator, Sustainer, & Savior Jesus Christ

Jim Muffo

Revelation 21:5

PublishAmerica
Baltimore

I love you, Uncle Jim,
Jim

U.R.
~ INCLUDED ~
REV 21:5

0%

© 2007 by Jim Muffo.
All rights reserved. No part of this book may be reproduced, stored in a retrieval system or transmitted in any form or by any means without the prior written permission of the publishers, except by a reviewer who may quote brief passages in a review to be printed in a newspaper, magazine or journal.

First printing

PublishAmerica has allowed this work to remain exactly as the author intended, verbatim, without editorial input.

All "Intro" Scriptures taken from THE MESSAGE//REMIX: The Bible in Contemporary Language, Copyright ©2003, 2006 by Eugene Petersen. Used by permission of NavPress Publishing Group.

Cover photos courtesy of Samantha Kleitz.

ISBN: 1-60441-084-1
PUBLISHED BY PUBLISHAMERICA, LLLP
www.publishamerica.com
Baltimore

Printed in the United States of America

ALL the Glory
ALL the Honor
&
ALL the Praise
to our
Creator, Sustainer, & Savior
Jesus Christ

It's ALL about Jesus; One Hundred Percent
It's ALL about His Life and His Righteousness
In Him I lack nothing; in Him I'm content
It's His Life or my life, no more and no less

It's ALL about Jesus; ALL things are by Him
He's Alpha, Omega; Beginning and End
He gets ALL the Glory; I don't get a thing
It's A/C or D/C; there's no in between

The General Epistle of James

"I, James, am a slave of God and the Master Jesus,
Writing to the twelve tribes scattered to Kingdom Come:
Hello!"

James 1:1
(The Message//Remix)

1/2   Count your blessings, my brethren, when temptations arise
      coming from all directions; that's the time to rejoice
3   Situations like this are more than trials or tests
      they are opportune moments to choose His Life instead

4   Just let go and trust Jesus; give His Life half a chance
      let His Life live without you in Complete Righteousness
5   If you ever lack Wisdom; go to God and just ask
      He will never rebuke you; He will always say "Yes!"

6   Rest assured He will do it; fix your focus on Him
      don't be doubtful or anxious, tossed like waves in the wind
7   Jesus says, "ALL or nothing; there is no in between
      trust in My Life completely, or I won't do a thing"

8   If you're one of those folks who wants the best of both worlds
      life won't have any meaning; it will all be up hill
9   To the brother in poverty, lift up your voice
      in His Life you lack nothing; praise the Lord and rejoice

10   To the brother who's wealthy; you who don't lack a thing
      if your trust is in riches, you will soon leave the scene
11   Like the flower that withers in the sun's scorching heat
      someday soon you will vanish; you'll be fully decreased

12   Jesus snuffs out temptation, drops it dead in its tracks
      He has promised His Life to anyone who will ask
13   When temptations oppress you, don't say "God's tempting me"
      God is Holy and Righteous; He does not work that way

14 Those temptations are brought on by your own wicked lust
   rising up to seduce you, to deceive and destruct
15 If this lust is then nourished, it will give birth to sin
   sin will reign till it's finished, leave you nothing but death

16 Do not falter my brethren; don't look right, don't look left
   place no trust in your own life; trust in His Life instead
17 Every excellent gift comes from the Father above
   He is always consistent; He is not changeable

18 Jesus made it ALL happen; brought us into His Life
   we are His new creations; we're His first rays of Light
19 Consequently, my brethren, let us open our ears
   close our mouths and just listen, with all anger deferred

20 Choose the fruits of His Spirit; cling to His Righteousness
   in His Life there's no vengeance, there is no fighting back
21 Therefore, lose ALL the cheap, shabby, vile wickedness
   stop pretending you're something; it is ALL about Him

22 Choose His Life every moment; leave your life at the Cross
   there is Only One Entrance to the Kingdom of God
23 He will trade you His Life at any moment you choose
   He is willing, but He always leaves the choice up to you

24 If you're still into thinking it's a relationship
   then your faith is still grounded in the law of sin and death
25 If you have His Life, live it! Don't go trading it back!
   you can hold on forever to His Infinite Gift

26 If you claim to have His Life, but you can't hold your tongue
   your religion is worthless; it is nothing but dung
27 Jesus does it without you; in Him, God is well pleased
   He serves orphans and widows in their hour of need

2/1   Trust in His Life, my brethren; live in His Righteousness
in His Life there's no bias; there is no prejudice
2   Do you classify people as "who's who" or "who's not"?
do you base your opinion on possessions or looks?

3   Do you make every effort to impress the "who's who"?
do you make every effort to ignore the "who's not"?
4   If you do, then His Life is not preeminent yet
your life still lives within you; you are still in the flesh

5   Listen up, my dear brethren; have you heard what God's done?
He has moved all these losers from the back to the front!
6   How could you have abused them? What did they do to you?
the "who's who" are the tyrants; they're the ones who are cruel

7   They're the ones who scream "Nonsense!" when you mention the Cross
they call Jesus a fable; they call Jesus a "crutch"
8   Jesus says, "Love ALL others, just as much as yourself"
let Him love them without you; if you do, you do well

9   If you choose to be partial; if you don't love them ALL
in God's eyes you're a rebel; you are breaking His Law
10 If you love ALL the others, but you still hate just one
you're still living in darkness; you have not seen the Son

11 God said, "Don't do adultery"; God said, "Thou shalt not kill"
if you're chaste, but you murder; you're His enemy still
12 If your words and your actions are inspired by Him
He will never condemn you; you'll be judged innocent

13 If you show no compassion, then your future is grim
let those bygones be bygones; lighten up and forgive
14 Don't just talk about Jesus; we all know talk is cheap
Jesus won't live inside you and not do anything

15 You have brothers and sisters who are hungry and cold
   longing for a hot meal and a warm set of clothes
16 If you say, "May God bless you; may you be warmed and filled"
   but don't feed them or clothe them; there's no Jesus in you

17 Stop the shallow lip-service; drop the self-righteous chat
   if you're not serving others, you're a cheap counterfeit
18 Faith and Works come together; precious gifts sent from Him
   you cannot separate them; they are sent hand-in-hand

19 You believe there is only one God, you do well
   demons also believe this; they're still trembling in hell
20 Use the brain God has given you; come on! use your head!
   can't you see that your words without actions are dead?

21 God called Abraham righteous; do you want to know why?
   he believed God enough to offer up Isaac's life
22 Faith and Works bond together; they pursue the same goal
   you cannot remove one without killing them both

23 Righteousness was imputed; Faith the means, Works the end
   it is written, God said it; "Abraham is My friend"
24 Faith and Works are the two keys that unlock Righteousness
   God has joined them together; God has made them "one flesh"

25 God pronounced Rahab righteous, a low-down prostitute
   when by her faith and works she hid the spies on her roof
26 Sever body and spirit, you have physical death
   separate Faith and Works, you have spiritual death

3/1   Let me warn you, my brethren, who are eager to teach
   there's a whole lot more to it than what you might first think
2 Those of us who are teachers, we make many mistakes
   what can make you or break you are the words that you say

3 Just by putting a small bit in the mouth of a horse
   we can make him obey us; keep him true to our course
4 A large ship can be guided through tempestuous winds
   by a very small rudder in a skilled skipper's hands

5 Though the tongue is so little, it can make a huge mark
   you can cause an explosion with just one tiny spark
6 In the body, the tongue is the most volatile part
   careless words can wreak havoc, set your whole world on fire

7. Every creature created in the animal world:
   mammals, birds, fish and reptiles, under man are subdued
8 But the tongue is rebellious with a life of its own
   it is toxic and deadly; it cannot be controlled

9 In one breath we are blessing God our Father above
   in the next breath we're swearing that our neighbor's a klutz
10 How can blessing and cursing both roll off the same tongue?
   this is serious my brethren; this just has to be stopped

11 When you turn on the spigot and you draw a cool drink
   is what comes out half water, mixed with half toxic waste?
12 Can a plum tree bear grapes or can a grapevine bear plums?
   you will never find water that is both hard and soft

13 Are you looking for answers? Do you want to be wise?
   let His Life live without you; never once compromise
14 Do you have any conflict or jealousy in your mind?
   don't proclaim you have His Life; don't pretend and don't lie

15 Strife and envy are products of the works of the flesh
   when God sees you, He sees you in complete lawlessness
16 When you grudge and you covet; when you quarrel and fight
   this all leads to disorder and a miserable life

17 His Life's Totally Other, just like midnight and Noon
    Jesus Christ is the Tree of Life; He's loaded with Fruit!
18 Anyone can have His Life; it's a simple exchange
    no disqualifications, just a whole lot of faith

4/1   Where do all of your conflicts, spats and quarrels come from?
    all your dissatisfaction comes from your vicious lust
2 You are selfish and greedy, you crave all that you see
    you would kill if you had to, still you cannot obtain

3 All your prayers are self-centered; they are "ALL about ME"
    "Self" is still your Dictator; Jesus Christ is decreased
4 If you still are self-centered; ALL about "#1"
    you are still God's opponent; you're still fighting the Son

5 Do you think God was lying, when in scripture He said
    "There is never contentment in the spirit of man"
6 If you still are disgruntled; if you're still not content
    lay your life on the altar; trust in His Life instead

7 Let His Life live without you; there is no other way
    He's your Armor of Righteousness, your Light and your Strength
8 Go to God and just ask Him to reveal His Son
    if you trust Him completely, it will surely be done

9 Recognize that you're hopeless; lose your cheap, worthless pride
    yes you must hit rock-bottom, you must be crucified
10 Fall in reverence before Him; just collapse at His feet
    He will instantly lift you; you'll be fully complete

11 When you spread ugly rumors, and when you criticize
    you've declared, "I'm the judge here;" you have snuffed out His Life
12 You have quickly forgotten that it's ALL about Him
    He's the King, Judge and Jury; the Beginning and End

13 You who plan out your strategies, year after year
   making all the smart moves to make your future secure
14 This is pride at its utmost; this is blind arrogance
   like spectacular fireworks, you're just smoke in the air

15 Its OK to be prudent, diligent in your plans
   just say, "If God is willing, I will do this or that"
16 As it is now, you act like you're in total control
   "I'M the Boss; I'M in charge here"; may God pity your soul

17 Give Him ALL of the Glory; don't hold anything back
   He must take you to zero; He accepts nothing less
5/1   One more word to the wealthy; you who think you're "all that"
   bawl your eyes out and bellow for what's right up ahead

2 All your gold, all your diamonds; all your stocks, bonds and cash
  all your vain gaudy "bling-bling" will be gone in a Flash
3 All your earthly possessions, all that made you so great
  they'll consume you like cancer; they will seal your fate

4 Look at all your employees you have duped and short-changed
  you thought no one was watching; Jesus sees everything!
5 You have lived in extravagance, reckless and loose
  you have caused untold damage, suffering and abuse

6 You've convicted and murdered lots of His precious saints
  they've all gone down in silence to their too-early graves
7 But in spite of this madness, God is still in control
  when the time comes for harvest, He will even the score

8 So relax, it's ALL finished! Just a matter of time!
  Jesus Christ is soon coming, in the blink of an eye
9 Drop the grudges, my brethren; just shake hands and forgive
  Judgment Day's fast approaching; Judgment Day is a Man!

10 All the prophets, my brethren; those who spoke for the Lord
   they were tortured and killed, but they stayed true to their course
11 Have you stopped to consider God's devout servant Job?
   he is one of the pillars in the Kingdom of God

12 Most importantly, brethren, drop those ungodly oaths
   to avoid condemnation, just say yes or say no
13 Are you tired and discouraged? then just do the exchange
   if you've already done it, lift your voice up in praise

14 If you're sick, if you're dying; call for those in His Life
   they will pray to the Father; He will open your eyes
15 If there's Faith, then the Works won't be too far behind
   there is no situation that can hinder His Life

16 Choose His Life every moment, then go out and make peace
   pray for ALL of your brethren; let Him live in your place
17 Now consider Elijah; just one man, yes, just one
   when he prayed, all the rain stopped for forty-two months

18 When he stood on Mount Carmel, just one man prayed again
   angry clouds brought a downpour, backed by blustery winds
19 Brethren tell ALL who'll listen, ALL about the exchange
   let His Love lead them to Him; let His Life show the way

20 Rest assured He will do it; let His Love draw them in
   He'll redeem them and lift them from a mountain of sin
   He is building His Kingdom, one exchange at a time
   there is only One Way, and that Way is His Life!

The First Epistle General of Peter

"I, Peter, am an apostle on assignment by Jesus, the Messiah, writing to exiles scattered to the four winds. Not one is missing, not one forgotten. God the Father has His eye on each one of you, and has determined by the work of the Spirit to keep you obedient through the sacrifice of Jesus. May everything good from God be yours!"

1 Peter 1:1, 2
(The Message // Remix)

1/3   Blessed be God the Father of our Lord Jesus Christ
       He has given us hope by raising Jesus to Life
4   Jesus offers us His Life, undefiled by sin
     we don't merit or earn it; it is His Precious Gift

5   It's His Life that sustains us; Jesus lives in our place
     Jesus does it without us, every step of the way
6   In His Life we're rejoicing; in His Life we're content
     though there's trials and troubles, in His Life we're at rest

7   All these many temptations are for His Life no match
     when it's all said and done with, only His Life will last
8   Though you've never seen Jesus, you've experienced His Life
     His Love wells up within you with unspeakable Joy

9   This New Life you've encountered, it's Eternal and Free!
     to retain it, all you must do is choose to believe
10 All God's prophets before you, all those great men of old
     they desired the "big picture", but they never were shown

11 They were told of Messiah; not told "who," "where," or "when"
     they just knew He would suffer and then rise up again
12 We have seen the fulfillment of ALL these prophecies
     Now His Spirit has shown us things that angels don't see

13 Time to put on our thinking caps and tune-up our minds
     realize that the Kingdom of God is His Life!
14 If His Life lives within us; if in us Jesus dwells
     we won't waste one more second looking out for ourselves

15 Choose His Life every moment; there is no other way
   Jesus living without you, every hour, every day
16 It is written, God said it; "Choose My Life and believe
   In My Life you are Holy; leave it ALL up to Me"

17 If you call on the Father, He will open your eyes
   He'll reveal His Son and you'll be offered His Life
18 His Life cannot be purchased; it is Free without price
   far above all religion; far beyond the "christ-like"

19 Jesus Christ was the only man who never once sinned
   by His death we were rescued; by His Life we now live
20 All His Life, Jesus did the Father's Ultimate Will
   They had ALL this planned out before creating the world

21 Jesus Christ was just like us; human flesh, human blood
   now His Life is Eternal; give ALL Glory to God!
22 Since we've opted for His Life; since we've done the exchange
   we love others with His Love; Love we can't imitate

23 By this New Life in Jesus, we are born once again
   it's His Life and His Only! It is ALL about Him!
24 All the rest of our lives are temporary as grass
   we are here for a short time, then we too quickly pass

25 His Life lives on forever! This, my friends, is Good News!
   He will trade you His Life at any moment you choose
2/1   Therefore, lose all the hatred; drop the lies and deceit
   stop the gossiping tongues and bury all jealousy

2 You experienced His Life when you believed what you heard
   choose His Life every moment; keep obeying His Word
3 Once you spend just one minute in His Glorious New Life
   you become living proof that He is gracious and kind

4   Jesus is our Foundation; the True Source of Real Life
    though the world crucified Him, God has set Him on High
5   ALL of us who choose His Life, we are His building blocks
    He's increasing His Kingdom, using each one of us

6   It is written, God said it; "I will build on this Stone
    ALL who trust My Foundation, they will never go wrong"
7   His Life's precious and priceless to ALL those who believe
    to ALL those who reject Him, He's a Rock, just the same

8   Over this Rock they'll stumble; He will stand in their way
    like He said, "I'll offend those who refuse to obey"
9   ALL of you who have His Life, you've been chosen by Him
    tell the whole world about this brand New Life you now live

10 Tell them how He redeemed you from your old dead-end life
    tell them how He delivered you from darkness to Light
11 My beloved, I beg you; pay no mind to this world
    don't be fooled into thinking that it's ALL about you

12 Let His Life shine on ALL your family, neighbors and friends
    when they see His Life in you, they will glorify Him
13 If His Life lives without you, you will truly be blessed
    you'll submit to authority like good citizens

14 You'll obey all the laws in your state and your town
    you will speak well of all men, from the President on down
15 This will silence those rumors that you're some kind of freak
    when they see His Life in you, they will truly believe

16 Use your newly found freedom to live out your New Life
    don't go taking advantage of the poor and the blind
17 Show concern for your neighbors, love them ALL with His Love
    give Him ALL of the Glory, save back none for yourself

18 Servants, obey your masters; do what they ask of you
    no it doesn't depend on if they're kind or they're cruel
19 If while trusting in His Life, you're unfairly abused
    His Life's more than sufficient; He will carry you through

20 If you're guilty, your punishment will be well deserved
    if you're innocent, then just leave it ALL up to Him
21 His Life wins every battle; He's the same now as then
    He will live your life for you if you call upon Him

22 Only Jesus was Sinless; Righteousness is a Man!
    Only Jesus was Holy; Truth is also a Man!
23 When they cursed Him and beat on Him, He never fought back
    He just suffered in silence, left it ALL in God's hands

24 Jesus died for ALL sinners, when He died on the cross
    He gave up ALL He had to get back ALL that was lost
25 Long before we believed Him, we were part of His plan
    now that His Life is our Life, we are safe in His hand

3/1   All you wives who have husbands that do not yet believe
    trust in His Life to win them; let Him do it His way
2 They will know by your words and they will see by your deeds
    you have Something they're lacking; you have Something they need

3 Do not measure your beauty by your looks, shape, or hair
    don't rely on your wardrobe or the jewelry you wear
4 Let all outward appearance disappear into Him
    in God's Ultimate Kingdom, Real Beauty is a Man!

5 Holy women of old who lived and died before Christ
    they possessed inner beauty; they were true loyal wives
6 Sarah treated her husband Abraham with respect
    treat your husbands the same by being calm and content

7 Likewise, all of you husbands, love and cherish your wives
     lift them up and protect them; walk with them in His Life
8 Edify one another; let His Life set the pace
     live in His Life together, full of Mercy and Grace

9 There is no getting even; there are no arguments
     only blessing and harmony; peace and respect
10 If you choose to let His Life live each moment for you
     you won't badmouth your neighbor; you will speak only truth

11 You'll avoid and shun evil, you will always do right
     you will be a real blessing to everyone in your life
12 In His Life, God the Father blesses ALL that you do
     in your own life, He'll let you try and fail till you're through

13 If you're dwelling in His Life, you will never know fear
     though your enemies stalk you, you'll be safe and secure
14 Even if they abuse you, you'll be filled with His Joy
     any evil done to Him soon becomes null and void

15 Choose His Life every moment; sanctify your Lord God
     give Him ALL of the Glory; lose your life in the Son
16 If you're trusting in His Life, you will never once stray
     your accusers and critics will just fall by the way

17 Persecution's a blessing when you're doing His Will
     it is cruel and harassing when you're focused on self
18 Jesus Christ also suffered; He's been there, He's done that
     gave His Life to deliver us from sin, self, and death

19 When He cried, "It is finished!" prophecy was fulfilled
     He proclaims to creation, "I will make ALL things new!"
20 God showed mercy to Noah; God supplied an escape
     though it took him a century, his whole family was saved

21 God has chosen baptism as our present escape
   we trade our life for His Life; we confirm the exchange
22 His Life is our Salvation; it is ALL about Him
   in His Kingdom, He fills ALL things, One Hundred Percent

4/1　　Trade your life in for His Life; don't hold anything back
   come alive in His Wisdom; dwell in His Righteousness
2　You won't waste one more minute looking out for yourself
   ALL your focus will center on His Ultimate Will

3　Though we now proclaim Jesus, it was not long ago
   all that brought us to life was sex and drugs, rock and roll
4　Now our old buds are baffled; they can't figure us out
   they declare that we've lost it; they insist we've spun out

5　Soon they'll see the Big Picture; soon they'll ALL understand
   they will soon realize that Judgment Day is a Man
6　We embrace the same message preached from Adam on down
   Jesus Christ is The Answer; He's the Only Way Out!

7　Soon the game will be over; it will not be long now
   we are in the ninth inning, bases loaded, two outs
8　Time to bury the hatchet, show His Love to ALL men
   His Life's more than Sufficient to absorb ALL our sins

9　Fix your focus on others; be a true friend indeed
   quickly come to their rescue in their moment of need
10　If you have His Life, flaunt it! Let His Love flow through you
   they will see Transformation; they will want His Life too

11　Give His Life full dominion, keep back none for yourself
   let Him do it without you; He does not need your help!
12　If hard times come upon you, never give up on God
   He is right there beside you; He is still on the job

13 Jesus knows when you're suffering, He has traveled that road
   when His Kingdom's established, Joy will flood through your soul
14 If they call you a dimwit for believing in Christ
   count it ALL as a blessing; stay secure in His Life

15 If you kill, steal, or meddle in your neighbor's affairs
   you deserve to be punished; you must pay for your errors
16 But if you suffer punishment for Jesus Christ's sake
   give Him ALL of the Glory; never once feel ashamed

17 Everyone will be judged for all they've done in the flesh
   He will start with believers, then He'll judge all the rest
18 Only one thing will save us; it's His Almighty Grace
   those who chose to reject Him will regret their mistake

19 Therefore, ALL who are suffering abuse for His Name
   rest assured, He will never reverse the exchange
5/1   I urge all you church elders, hear these words that I say
   this same Jesus they murdered; He is now King of Kings!

2 Tend His flock like real shepherds; nurture His lambs and sheep
   don't exploit them or fleece them, like some cheap hireling
3 Never once fool yourself by thinking they are your own
   they belong to the Master; ALL of them, yes, each one

4 On that Glorious Day when we behold Jesus Christ
   you'll be greatly rewarded if you've treated them right
5 Those of you who are younger, show your elders respect
   those of you who are older, always put others first

6 If you love and serve others with His Perfect Love
   He will highly exalt you in the Kingdom of God
7 ALL your fears; ALL your worries; ALL your anxieties
   you can lose them this instant, through a simple exchange

8 Chose His Life every moment; give the devil no chance
   to seduce and deceive and lure you into his trap
9 He's already defeated; there will be no rematch
   to ALL you who know Jesus; Victory is a Man!

10 ALL of us who have chosen to embrace this exchange
   we will soon be exactly what He meant us to be
11 Yes, our Lord Jesus Christ is our Beginning and End
   our Creator, our Sustainer, our Savior; Amen!

12 My dear brother, Silvanus, brings this letter to you
   I've been careful to tell you ALL I know to be true
13 Everyone here sends greetings to each one of you
   we're ALL in Him together; Mark, my son, says "Hi" too

14 Love each other with His Love; live in peace with ALL men
   Thank You for Your Life, Jesus! Hallelujah! Amen!

The Second Epistle General of Peter

"I, Simon Peter, am a servant and apostle of Jesus Christ: I write this to you whose experience with God is as life-changing as ours, all due to our God's straight dealing and the intervention of our God and Savior, Jesus Christ. Grace and peace to you many times over as you deepen in your experience with God and Jesus our Master."

II Peter 1:1, 2
(The Message//Remix)

3 ALL we need to please the Father is ALL wrapped up in His Son
   Jesus is the One Eternal Life that's free to everyone!
4 What a great and precious promise! What a Glorious Escape!
   we can trade our life for His Life through immediate exchange

5 Each exchange gives Him the chance to do what only He can do
   He's our Virtue, He's our Knowledge; we add nothing to the soup
6 Jesus never once is anxious; Jesus always is content
   Jesus never strays or stumbles; Jesus IS the Narrow Path!

7 Jesus focuses on others; He's attentive to their needs
   He will bless you with His Perfect Love if you will just believe
8 Each exchange is for the moment; every moment you must choose
   every moment spent in His Life brings forth Everlasting Fruit

9 Each reversal lands you right back in the law of sin and death
   always striving, always struggling, never finding time to rest
10 Therefore listen up, my brethren; this is ALL so cut and dried
   ALL you have to "do" is trust Him; He will fill you with His Life

11 Now when Jesus lives without you, you are living in His Grace
   He is Holy, He is Righteous; Jesus IS the Narrow Gate!
12 I know everyone has heard this all a million times before
   if the Son is living in you-you're Complete! you need no more!

13 Just wake up and smell the coffee; open up your sleepy eyes
   I'm so happy to inform you, night is gone-you're in the Light!
14 Everybody stop and listen; I don't have that much time left
   I am near my destination; I will soon be filled by Him

15 When I'm dead and gone I hope that you'll remember what I've said
   yes, the only thing that you can "do" is choose His Life instead
16 Jesus was a real person, not some children's fairy tale
   I have seen Him do things that nobody ever did before

17 We all heard the Father's voice from heaven, seems like yesterday
   saying, "This is My Beloved Son, in whom I am well pleased"
18 Ask James and John; we all were there; we all heard the same thing
   we saw Him as the Son of God; we've never been the same

19 Are you groping in the darkness? You can see the Son today!
   choose His Life this very moment; He will trade you instantly
20 I am not just speculating; no, this IS the Gospel Truth
   I received it straight from Jesus; now I'm sharing it with you

21 God showed His prophets Light when He decided they should see
   The Spirit told them what to write; they never changed a thing
2/1   There were "wannabees" back then and there are "wannabees" today
   if their message isn't Jesus Christ Alone; it's heresy!

2 We hear many many teachers teaching many many things
   though they talk a lot about Him, Christ in nowhere in their game
3 They'll seduce you with their doctrines; they will beg and they will plead
   they'll convince you, then they'll fleece you; they will harvest all your seeds

4 Look what God did to the angels, ALL the angels that rebelled
   He delivered them to darkness; He has cast them down to hell
5 Look what God did to this earth when He put Noah in the ark
   everything was terminated in those forty day and nights

6 Look at Sodom and Gomorrah; into ashes they were turned
   God put evil through the Fire; what a lesson to be learned!
7 Though Lot also lived in Sodom, he did not condone their sin
   all their wickedness distressed him, therefore God delivered him

8   Lot lived right downtown on Main Street; day by day he was disturbed
    he saw every evil deed and he heard every filthy word
9   God delivers ALL His children from temptation through His Son
    He allows the wicked lots of rope until it's time to judge

10 God sees ALL these headstrong rebels; He sees ALL their discontent
    always ripping on their leaders; arrogant and quick to vent
11 Even angels up in heaven who have way more power than them
    they don't slander or accuse them; they don't judge, they don't condemn

12 ALL these self-appointed prophets and the heresies they preach
    they will soon pass through the Fire; they'll be totally decreased
13 They won't live one second longer than their expiration date
    they'll go down just like the rowdy and disturbers of the peace

14 ALL their lust for power, wealth and fame, and ALL the lies they've told
    ALL their formulas and strategies will soon go up in smoke
15 These are followers of Balaam; they are rotten to the core
    yes it's ALL about the money; nothing less and nothing more

16 Balaam finally got the message, finally saw his foolishness
    God enabled Balaam's donkey to rebuke him for his sin
17 ALL these teachers are abandoned wells; they're filthy clouds of smog
    they're descending into darkness; they just want to drag you down

18 They claim God will make you rich if you will only plant the seed
    they have duped a lot of Christians by appealing to their greed
19 "If you want to know "The Answer," buy my books and DVD's!
    just call 888-whatever", these are money-hungry thieves

20 Once you've tasted Real Freedom, but then throw it all away
    you'll end up in greater bondage, bound by even bigger chains
21 You'd be better off if you had never once done the exchange
    better never to exchange than to reverse and walk away

22 Listen to King Solomon, the wisest man who ever lived
   you'll be like a cleaned up dog who wallows in his puke again
3/1   This is now my second letter I am sending out to you
   it contains the same old message; nothing added, nothing new

2 ALL God's prophets long ago and ALL His messengers today
   they've delivered this same message that I presently proclaim
3 In the last days, lots of sly, smooth-talking serpents will pop up
   they will lure you, they'll seduce you, seek to undermine your trust

4 They will say, "If Christ is truly coming, why is He so late?"
   when I see it, I'll believe it; let Him show Himself today!"
5 They've conveniently forgotten that ALL things exist through Him
   He spoke everything from nothing; ALL things get their start from Him

6 When He judged the world the first time, he just spoke and it was done
   He destroyed the earth with water; purified it through the flood
7 When He comes to judge the world again, the effect will be more dire
   He'll absorb ALL things back into Him; He will purify with Fire

8 My beloved, don't be foolish; He won't come one minute late
   one day is to Him a thousand years; a thousand years, a day
9 He won't stall or dilly-dally; He will show up right on time
   He has blessed us ALL with extra time to believe and choose His Life

10 He will come back in an instant; He will roll away the sky
   He'll dissolve the air and water; He will purge the earth with Fire
11 Here today and gone tomorrow, folks; it's time to take a stand
   trust His Life this very moment, then just choose His Life instead

12 Rest securely in His promise; fix your focus ALL on Him
   He will bring you through the Fire; you will then be filled by Him
13 We don't listen to the scoffers, we don't pay them any mind
   we believe our King is coming; we believe it's nearly time!

14 Therefore, ALL my dear beloved, come to Jesus; live in Peace
   don't let anyone discourage you; He'll be here any day
15 God is patient, God is waiting; giving everyone a chance
   our beloved brother Paul confirms that I am right on this

16 When some folks read his epistles, they're bewildered and perplexed
   they contort and twist his teachings into what is best for them
17 Therefore, ALL my dear beloved, put ALL vanity aside
   Fix your focus ALL on Jesus; just keep trusting in His Life

   He will sanctify you more and more as you choose to obey
   He'll give you His Eternal Life each time that you exchange

The First Epistle General of John

"From the very first day, we were there, taking it all in. We heard it with our ears, saw it with our own eyes, verified it with our own hands. The Word of Life appeared right before our eyes, we saw it happen! And now we're telling you in most somber prose that what we witnessed was, incredibly, this: The Infinite Life of God Himself took shape before us."

I John 1:1, 2
(The Message//Remix)

1/3 We have seen it, we have heard it; we are passing it along
     it's a Gift to everybody from the Father and the Son
4   We have written all these things so every one of you will know
     when you trade your life for His Life, you'll find Joy you've never known!

5   Yes, this is our "Good News!" message; yes, we got it straight from Him
     we're in the Light—in Jesus Christ—in Him there is no sin
6   If we claim we have His Life but we still live in selfishness
     we are lying; we are walking in the law of sin and death

7   ALL of us who've chosen His Life dwell in perfect fellowship
     Jesus lives in every one of us; His blood absorbs our sins
8   If we claim that we're "good people," we have been too badly fooled
     our deceitful hearts have duped us; we've been lured away from Truth

9   If we openly admit that we are sinners, He'll forgive
     He'll redeem us; He will cleanse us ALL from ALL unrighteousness
10 If we say that we have never sinned, we really miss the mark
     we deny Him, we reject Him; we declare that He's a liar

2/1 My dear children, I implore you, choose His Life; exchange with Him
     if you stumble and reverse it, He'll exchange with you again
2   Only Jesus has Eternal Life; it's ALL wrapped up in Him!
     He'll exchange His Life with anyone who trusts and chooses Him

3   We can know we have His Life beyond a shadow of a doubt
     just obey Him; just exchange with Him; let Jesus do it ALL!
4   Any man who says, "I know Him," but does not do the exchange
     he is lying; no Truth in him; he's refusing to obey

5   Any man who chooses His Life, then remains in the exchange
    he will blossom, he will flourish; he'll display Amazing Grace
6   If a man claims he has His Life, there's a simple way to tell
    he'll display His Perfect Love and love his neighbor as himself

7   Brethren, there is nothing new here; same old message, nothing's changed
    all the way from Genesis till now, it's always been the same
8   There's been only one thing added after Jesus went away
    it's been with us since Pentecost; we now have the exchange

9   If a man says he is in the Light, but hates his brother still
    he's still blind and he's still groping; he's in darkness even now
10 If a man loves ALL his brothers, you will know he's in His Life
    he'll love them ALL; he'll never fall; he'll always treat them right

11 If a man loves ALL his brothers, but still hates just even one
    that man's still blind in both his eyes; in darkness he is lost
12 I am writing to you, little children; hear me when I say
    ALL your sins have been forgiven, and it's ALL for His Name's Sake!

13 I am writing to the fathers who have known Him all along
    I am writing to the sons who in His Life have overcome
14 He's defeated Satan for you; in your weakness He is strong
    Yes, we ALL come to the Father by exchanging with the Son

15 Do not love those worldly ways and things; don't make them "#1"
    If you do, the Father's not in you and neither is the Son
16 All the best this world can offer: all the power, wealth, and fame,
    none of this is from the Father; soon these things will pass away

17 Soon the world and all its lust for more will vanish into Him
    those who trade for His Eternal Life will always be content
18 Little children, time is very short; you've heard of antichrist
    he's already here; he's everywhere; he doesn't have much time

19 All those bright lights that blew out were never really bright at all
   they were look-a-likes and counterfeits; just cheap, generic bulbs
20 ALL of you have the anointing; ALL of you have the exchange
   Jesus Christ is now your Wisdom; in His Life, you know ALL things!

21 I did not write this because I thought you didn't know the Truth
   I just wanted to remind you, there are liars on the loose
22 These deceivers all swear up and down that Jesus wasn't Christ
   they deny the Father and the Son; they refuse to see the Light

23 Whosoever rejects Jesus, he rejects the Father too
   whosoever accepts Jesus, he receives the Father too
24 Trust in His Life every moment; choose His Life all through the day
   if you want to please the Father, Jesus IS the Only Way!

25 He has made a special promise to ALL those who will believe
   In His Life we'll ALL live on and on for ALL eternity!
26 I have written you this letter so that all of you will know
   all these tricksters, frauds and swindlers want to keep you from the Truth

27 Jesus Christ is your Foundation, your Strong Tower of Defense
   He will teach you, you need no one else; put ALL your faith in Him!
28 Little children, just keep trusting; just keep doing the exchange
   when He comes in ALL His Glory, you'll be thrilled and not ashamed

29 Jesus IS the One Eternal Life; The Way! The Life! The Truth!
   If you trust His Life completely, He will do it ALL for you!
3/1 We're now children of the Father; what Amazing Awesome Love!
   to the world, we're nothing special; they have not yet seen the Son

2 My beloved, though we're Sons of God, we ain't seen nothing yet
   When He comes, He will transform us; we will see Him as He is
3 Jesus IS the Hope within us; in His Virtue, we're secure
   Jesus does it ALL without us; it's His Life that makes us pure

4   Self-dependence, self-reliance, self-sufficiency is sin
    these things war against the Spirit, make His Life of no effect
5   Jesus didn't come to earth to show and tell us how to live
    Jesus came to be our Life; He came to be our Righteousness

6   Whosoever trusts in Jesus, God sees him as innocent
    he who trusts in self is groping in the law of sin and death
7   Little children, we know better; no we won't get fooled again
    our religion is just filthy rags; our Righteousness is Him!

8   He who puts his faith in self obeys the Father of ALL lies
    Jesus came for just one reason, to speak darkness into Light
9   Anyone who now has His Life will from ALL their striving cease
    In His Life there is no struggling; in His Life there's Victory

10 Here's the way to tell the difference between His Life and the rest
    ALL disharmony is evil and ALL discontent is sin
11 Love each other! Hear His Message! This is what our Lord commands!
    it's His Law since the beginning; it's His Law until the end

12 Cain jealously killed Abel when his offering was not blessed
    he kept his best back for himself, but Abel gave his best
13 Brethren, do not be astonished if the world calls you a geek
    they will mock you, they will hate you; they'll say you're some kind of freak

14 That's OK, we ALL know better; we're ALL in His Perfect Love
    we just pray; "Father, forgive them; they have not yet seen the Son"
15 Whosoever hates his brother is a murderer indeed
    he has traded Life Eternal for an expiration date

16 Jesus came to earth and gave His ALL to win back ALL of us
    we look out for one another; we display His Perfect love
17 If you have the means to help but you ignore your neighbors needs
    you're still focused on yourself; His Life is nowhere on the scene

18 Little children, His Love separates the Real from the fake
   if it's Jesus living in us, we will practice what we preach
19 If we practice what we preach, then there will be Abundant Fruit
   This is how He reassures us and confirms us in the Truth

20 Jesus overcomes ALL worry; Jesus overthrows ALL doubt
   Jesus Christ knows ALL the answers; in His Life it's ALL worked out
21 My beloved, if we're living in His Perfect Righteousness
   we can come before the Throne of God in total confidence

22 If we're keeping His commandments; if our focus is on Him
   if we lose our life for His Life, we'll receive ALL that we ask
23 This is ALL so very simple; He has only two commands
   believe Jesus is the Son of God and love your fellow men

24 If we're keeping His commandments; if we're dwelling in His Life
   we'll possess His Holy Spirit; He'll possess out hearts and minds
4/1 My beloved, heed my warning; don't believe all that you hear
   there are many bogus prophets running wild everywhere

2 ALL the prophets sent from God declare that Jesus is His Son
   they proclaim that God came down to earth in human flesh and blood
3 ALL the prophets that deny this Truth are feeding you a lie
   they are wolves in sheep's attire; they're the troops of antichrist

4 We have God, my little children; in His Life we overcome
   nothing in this world can fool us; Jesus lives instead of us
5 All these messengers of darkness preaching all their common sense
   they will lure you, they'll deceive you; they are very smooth with words

6 We preach Jesus Christ and nothing else; He IS the Only Truth!
   ALL believers understand this; unbelievers call us fools
7 My beloved, let us love each other with His Perfect Love
   We're ALL in His Life together; in His Life we now know God

8   He who doesn't love his neighbor, that man doesn't yet know God
      it's impossible to know Him and not show His Perfect Love
9   Perfect Love was demonstrated when the Father sent His Son
      down to earth to live among us; down to earth to rescue us

10 Here is Perfect Love in action; no we didn't first love Him
      He first loved us and He sent His Son to nullify our sins
11 My beloved, what Amazing Grace! How Awesome is our God!
      we can't help but freely love each other with His Perfect Love

12 There's not one of us who've ever seen the Father face to face
      if we truly love each other, Jesus loves them in our place
13 This is how we know for certain we've experienced the exchange
      we love everyone with His Love; Love we cannot imitate

14 We have seen Him; we proclaim Him Jesus is no fairy tale
      God the Father sent His Son to be the Savior of the world
15 Whosoever shall confess that Jesus is the Son of God
      you can know God lives within him; you can know he's seen the Son

16 We now know it and believe beyond a shadow of a doubt
      God IS Love; we have received Him; Jesus lives instead of us
17 We don't worry about Judgment Day; we're ALL secure in Him
      Jesus lives our lives without us; in His Life we have no sin

18 In His Life we're not afraid; His Love removes anxiety
      when we worry, we're tormented; we have not done the exchange
19 We give Jesus ALL the Glory; ALL the Honor; ALL the praise
      we now love Him cause He loved us while we still were enemies

20 If a man claims he loves God, but hates his brother, it's not true
      how can he love the Creator and not love His creatures too?
21 Just remember the commandment that we ALL received from Him
      "If you really love Me, you will also love your fellow man"

5/1　　Now whoever believes Jesus is the Christ, is born of God
　　　those who truly love the Father, they will also love His Son
2　If we love God, we'll obey Him; we'll let Jesus do it ALL
　　we will then love ALL His precious children with His Perfect Love

3　We now show our love for God by doing ALL that He commands
　　He has made it simple so that anyone can understand
4　Those who trade their life for His Life, they have overcome the world
　　they're Victorious by faith in Jesus Christ and nothing else!

5　There is Only One Way to escape from pride and discontent
　　come to Jesus, put your trust in Him; exchange your life for His
6　Jesus Christ came to redeem us through His birth and through His death
　　we believe it; by the Spirit, who has verified all this

7　There are Three in heaven that agree in Perfect Unison
　　God the Father, and the Word, and Holy Ghost; these Three are One
8　There are three on earth who join together to confirm the Son
　　by His birth, His death, His resurrection; we're now right with God

9　We believe man's testimony when just two or three agree
　　God is greater than a million men; He's spoken-we believe
10　Those abiding in the Son now have His Life as living proof
　　unbelievers label God a liar by disregarding Truth

11　God has given us a Great Escape from sin and self and death
　　there is Only One Eternal Life! Jesus possesses it!
12　Those who've traded lives with Jesus now have Life that never ends
　　those who blow Him off or try to help Him are still dead in sin

13　I have written ALL these things to you who in His Life abide
　　you can know today, through the exchange, you have Eternal Life!
14　Jesus Christ is our Assurance; there's no room for doubt or fear
　　when we pray according to His Will, we know He hears our prayers

15 And we know that since He hears us, He will honor our requests
   when we ask him to decrease us til there's nothing left but Him
16 When you see believers stumble, intercede to God for them
   He gives Light to ALL the humble; He blinds ALL the arrogant

17 We ALL stumble, no one's sinless; He's not finished with us yet
   but He's promised, "What I've started, I will surely bring to pass"
18 When we're in His Life, we're blameless, far beyond all wickedness
   we are Holy; we are Godly; we are in His Righteousness

19 We have seen His Life in action; we have ALL the proof we need
   we're not loaded down with anger, envy or anxiety
20 Jesus does it ALL without us, He's the One Eternal Life
   yes, His yoke is way too easy; yes, His burden's way too light!

21 Little children, listen to me; I am telling you the truth
   rid yourselves of ALL self-effort; let Him do it without you!
                           Amen

The Second Epistle of John

"My dear congregation, I, your pastor, love you in every truth.
And I'm not alone—
everyone who knows the truth that has taken up
permanent residence in us loves you"

II John 1: 1, 2
(The Message//Remix)

3 Grace and Mercy and Peace to ALL of you in His Life
   Truth and Love from the Father, through His Son Jesus Christ
4 I'm so happy to see that you've discovered The Way
   He's our Gift from the Father when we choose to obey

5 I now urge you, beloved; let Him live without you
   this is no new commandment; it is His Perfect Will
6 We know His Perfect Love when we obey His commands
   He's the Vine, we're the branches; Our New Life is in Him

7 Many teachers deny that Jesus came as our Life
   by their stubborn rejection, they become antichrist
8 Keep exchanging with Jesus; He will never reverse
   we will live for eternity in His Righteousness

9 ALL who settle for "christ-like", they are still on their own
   anyone who's exchanged has both the Father and Son
10 Any teacher whose teachings disallow the exchange
   don't receive him as family; do not bid him God speed

11 If you give him God's blessing, you've succumbed to his lies
   you've become his accomplice by denying His Life
12 I have much more to say, more than this letter can hold
   I will tell you in person; then our joy will be full

13 All of us who are here in His Life, in His Truth
    to all those there in His Life; warmest greetings to you!
                         Amen

The Third Epistle of John

"The pastor, to my good friend Gaius. How I truly love you! We're the best of friends, and I pray for good fortune in everything you do, and for good health-that your everyday affairs prosper, as well as your soul."

III John 1:1, 2
(The Message//Remix)

3 I rejoiced when they told me you are walking in Truth
   by your words and your actions, you've displayed Living Proof
4 There is no greater joy than to hear this good news
   I rejoice when my children function in His Life too

5 You've shown His Perfect love to friends and strangers alike
   they've seen Jesus in action; they have witnessed His Life
6 They reported back to us how you helped them along
   you provided provisions when they passed through your town

7 They were strangers among you, travelling in His Name
   unbelievers ignored them; they supplied them no aid
8 When you make them feel welcome, you exhibit His Life
   you supply bed and breakfast to the Body of Christ

9 I have written this to you, but now Di-ot're-phes
   in his own pious wisdom's taken issue with me
10 If I come there, I'll remember all he's said and done
   he's disfellowshipped folks who've traded lives with the Son

11 Don't be fooled, my dear brethren; this is ALL about Christ!
   in His Life you see clearly; in your life you are blind
12 Now concerning De-me'tri-us, he's done the exchange
   we know Truth when we see it; we know Jesus agrees

13 There are so many more things that I wanted to say
   but I just can't include them all with paper and ink
14 But I trust that, God willing, we'll soon meet face to face
   in His Peace we salute you; greet our friends there by name

The General Epistle of Jude

"I, Jude, am a slave to Jesus Christ and brother to James, writing to those loved by God the Father, called and kept safe by Jesus Christ. Relax, everything's going to be alright; rest, everything's coming together; open your hearts, Love is on the way!"

Jude 1:1, 2
(The Message//Remix)

3 My dear friends, I felt compelled to write to you about His Life
   now I urge you, keep exchanging; lose yourselves in Jesus Christ
4 There are phonies there among you; even now, this very hour
   they are godly imitations, but they still deny the Power

5 Though from Egypt, God provided Israel's deliverance
   by His Word, ALL unbelievers perished in the wilderness
6 ALL the discontented angels, ALL the ones who wanted more
   God has damned them ALL to darkness till He purges them with Fire

7 Even Sodom and Gomorrah and their fornicating ways
   God made them for our example; they remain fully decreased
8 Likewise, ALL these filthy dreamers, they are servants of the flesh
   they despise the legal system and they bash the government

9 Even Michael the archangel, when for Moses he was sent
   did not once rebuke the devil; he said, "God will handle this"
10 ALL these self-ordained apostles are like wild animals
   they're imbedded in the natural; infected and defiled

11 Woe to each and every one of them; like Cain, they've missed the mark
   they are greedy just like Balaam; they are rebels to the core
12 They are poisonous infections; they are bold and arrogant
   they are wind-blown clouds of thunder; barren trees whose roots are dead

13 They are raging waves of discontent, obsessed with earthly things
   they are meteors of evil with an expiration date
14 Even Enoch prophesied that we will ALL see Judgment Day
   "Listen up! The Lord is coming with ten thousands of His saints!"

15 In His Judgment, ALL created things will flow back into Him
   in His Presence, EVERY knee will bow and EVERY tongue confess
16 All these white-washed plastic Christians and their "can't miss" strategies
   all their seminars and conferences have brought them wealth and fame

17 But remember now, my brethren, the apostles were not wrong
   they received the truth from Jesus, then they passed it on to us
18 They foresaw these cheap imposters masquerading in His Name
   craving any scrap of glory they could grab along the way

19 These are creatures of rebellion, dead in disobedience
   they are hell-bent for destruction; they are walking in the flesh
20 You are different, dear brethren; by His Grace you've seen the Light
   you've asked Jesus to decrease you till there's nothing left but Christ

21 Never doubt, just keep exchanging; we know Mercy is a Man
   Jesus Christ is our Beginning, our Existence, and our End
22 Take it easy on the newborns; give those seeds some time to sprout
   let Him show them His Compassion; just let Jesus raise them up

23 Bring your sightless friends to Jesus; let them see what He can do
   He hates sin but loves the sinner; He'll convert them without you
24 Jesus Christ is our Foundation; He's the Rock on which we stand
   Jesus Christ is our Redeemer; our Eternal Life is Him!

25 Jesus Christ gets ALL the Glory; He is our Majestic King
   in His Power and Dominion, we'll ALL live eternally!
                            Amen

Jesus, live instead of me, now and through eternity
There is nothing I can do; it's entirely up to You
Everything that is of me, must be nailed to the tree
All that is of me must die; You Alone must crucify

You came to earth in human flesh; You lived in Perfect Righteousness
You took my place at Calvary; You died my death instead of me
You took my debt, You paid the price; You traded me Eternal Life
Because of You, I am complete; You walk the path instead of me

Day by day my cross I bear; Your Life's waiting for me there
Your Life knows the narrow path; Your life never once looks back
May Your Kingdom be increased; may Your Wonders never cease
Victory's already won; I stand Victorious in the Son!

"Come unto me, all ye that labor and are heavy laden, and I will give you rest. Take my yoke upon you and learn of me; for I am meek and lowly in heart; and ye shall find rest unto your souls. For my yoke is easy and my burden is light."

Matthew 11:28-30

I come to You Jesus, and sit at Your feet
in silence to hear every word that You speak
I bring no petition for unfulfilled need
in You I lack nothing; in You I'm complete

You are my Creator, my Savior, my King
my Joy, my Contentment, my Comfort, my Peace
My Shield, my Buckler, my Shelter from harm
my Courage, my Victory, my Rock in the storm

You're Alpha, Omega; Beginning and End
my Master, my Teacher, my Wisdom, my Friend
my Justification, my Mercy, my Grace
my Sanctification and my Righteousness

You willingly, joyfully went to the cross
You poured ALL your blood out for ALL that was lost
You went to the grave; You arose from the dead
You are my Atonement; You paid off my debt

Yes, you are The Way and The Truth and The Life
Your body's The Bread and Your blood is The Wine
Your Life is The Gate and Your Life is The Path
my life I abandon for Your Life instead

Yes, You must increase to One Hundred Percent
and You must decrease me till nothing is left
Your Ultimate Will is to live in my place
Eternal Salvation; Eternal Exchange

God loved us so much that He gave us His Son
in Jesus, it's finished! In Jesus, it's done!
His yoke is so easy, His burden so light
All Jesus requires, is "Trust in My Life!"

"Come now, and let us reason together," saith the Lord: "Though your sins be as scarlet, they shall be as white as snow; though they be red like crimson, they shall be as wool."

Isaiah 1:18

I met a man named Jesus Christ, a little while back
I thought I'd know Him all my life, but never quite like that
I knew a lot about Him, thought I had Him figured out
I never had the slightest clue what He is ALL about

He said, "I'm your Creator, your Sustainer, Lord, and Friend
In Me ALL things have their beginning; ALL things have their end
I knew you well a million years before creation week
I made you in My image, individually unique

I've been right here beside you every moment of your life,
just waiting for My chance to speak your darkness into Light
I know the end from the beginning; what was lost is found
I never once gave up on you; I knew you'd come around

I watched you every minute through those worthless, wasted years
I saw the the guilt, the grief, the shame, the worry, pain and fear
the anger, the resentment, the rebellion and the pride
I never once abandoned you; I never left your side

I knew someday you'd understand, you're nothing without Me
Without My Life, you're good as dead for ALL eternity
I AM the Only Way; I'm everything you'll ever need
I AM the Only Truth that will forever make you free

I AM the One and Only Life that will forever live
to anyone who trusts in Me, My Life I'll freely give
This is My Life; this is My Gift; to ALL who WILL believe
there is no cost; the price was paid in full at Calvary

It doesn't matter where you've been, or what you may have done
your sins are ALL forgotten once you finally see the Son
They're blotted out forever; I'll remember them no more
though they be red as scarlet, I will make them white as snow"

3   "Blessed is the man who places no trust in himself
    I'll fill him with My Spirit; in My Kingdom he will dwell
4   Blessed is the man who sees his hopeless state and grieves
    I'll bear him up on eagles wings throughout eternity

5   Blessed is the gentle man who puts his brother first
    I'll give him an eternal home when I remake the earth
6   Blessed is the man who wants My Life above ALL else
    I'll be his daily Bread and Wine; in Me he will be filled

7   Blessed is the man who will forgive abundantly
    I'll take his sins and cast them to the bottom of the sea
8   Blessed is the man whose heart is longing for My Grace
    I will not disappoint him; he will surely see My face

9   Blessed is the man whose top priority is peace
    I'll make him My beloved child for ALL eternity
10 Blessed is the man who's persecuted for My sake
    I'll set him in My Kingdom; I'm preparing him a place

11 Blessed is the man who suffers ridicule and shame
    the one who's made a laughingstock, by reason of My name
12 Rejoice, My child and shout for joy! The payoff will be great!
    they've always treated Mine like this; it's always been the same

13 You have My Life, now live it! Show the world just who I AM!
    if you go back to your life, you'll end up an "also ran"
14 I AM your Light, so let Me shine; this is My Perfect Will
    illuminating darkness like a city on a hill

15 So throw back all the curtains, and turn on all the lights
   I AM no secret to be kept; display Me far and wide
16 Be generous and freely share My Life with everyone
   just love them with My Perfect Love, and they will see the Son!"

Matthew 5:3-16

1 Though I speak as a man in a heavenly voice
    if it's not You who's talking, it's just cheap, worthless noise
2 Though I know every answer; though my faith mountains move
    if You are not my Wisdom, I am simply a fool

3 Though I die as a martyr; give my all to the poor
    if it's not You who's giving, there will be no reward
4 You are kind and long-suffering; You are humble and meek
    in Your Life there's no envy, vanity or conceit

5 Your behavior is upright; You put ALL others first
    You are patient, forbearing, never thinking the worst
6 You will never delight in anything I can do
    You will only rejoice when I am trusting in You

7 Your Life bears every burden; Your Life fills me with Faith
    Your Life holds me, assures me, every step of the way
8 You're my Rock, my Foundation; You Alone are my Strength
    all things done in my power will soon vanish away

9 Even though I may claim to know a lot about You
    I have not scratched the surface; I do not have a clue
10 Someday Your Life will fill me; I'll be fully decreased
    You will trade me Your Spirit for my flesh that's so weak

11 Back when I was a child, it was ALL about me
    now it's ALL about Jesus; He is ALL that I need
12 If it's not about Jesus, it's another dead end
    my Atonement, my Redemption, my Salvation is Him

13 Jesus, Your Life is my Life; You're the Faith I possess
You're the Hope I hold on to; You're the Love I express
These are Your Perfect Gifts sent from heaven above
but the greatest of these Gifts is Your Perfect Love

                I Corinthians 13

1 "He who trades his life for My Life; he who finds My Secret Place
   ALL his words, his thoughts, his actions, will originate in Me
2 He will say, "Your Life is my Life; my Protection, my Defense
   nothing in this world can faze me; in Your Life I calmly rest"

3 "I will clear away the evil traps that barricade his path
   I'll depress the epidemic that would seek to bring him death
4 I'll sustain him in My Presence; I will hold him in My hand
   I will be his Shield and Buckler; in My Truth he'll firmly stand

5 No disaster in the darkest night will make this man afraid
   no catastrophe in broad daylight will shake his trust in Me
6 No demonic devastation will remove him from his place
   no satanic plague will take him out; I AM his Great Escape

7 Though the dead lay all around him; though he see ten thousand fall
   I will spare him from destruction; I AM with him through it ALL
8 He will never face My Judgment; in My Life, he's innocent
   he'll only watch as all the lost receive their recompense

9 Because this man has placed his trust in Me and Me Alone
   I'll be his Everlasting Life; his Everlasting Home
10 No evil shall befall him; I'll subdue his every storm
   in My Life he will safely dwell; I'll shelter him from harm

11 I will send ten thousand angels, if indeed that's what it takes
   to prevent this man from falling as he journeys on his way
12 They'll bear him up on eagles wings, uphold him in My Grace
   they'll deliver him from danger; they'll protect him with My Strength

13 There is nothing in this world that can rise up and block his path
over lions, snakes and dragons, he'll securely, safely pass
14 Since he's chosen Me above ALL else, I'll bring him through the Fire
he will sit with Me in heaven; I will honor his desire

15 When he calls, I'll always answer; I will never leave his side
I'll redeem him from destruction; in My Glory he'll abide
I will be his Life Eternal; he'll forever be My Friend
he will flourish in My Kingdom; in My Life that never ends"

Psalm 91

18 Preach the Cross to the worldly, they will laugh in your face
   but to those who know Jesus, it is Almighty Grace
19 It is written, God said it; "Human wisdom I'll quell
   I will make the wise stupid, all the experts dispel"

20 ALL the knowledge existing in the world's hall of fame
   God has made it ALL nonsense; good-for-nothing and lame
21 Since the world in its wisdom chose to set God aside
   He ordained foolish preaching to bring sinners to Life

22 Jews desire signs and wonders, they demand miracles
   Greeks prefer validation, backed by logical proof
23 We preach Jesus Christ crucified; nothing more, nothing less
   to the Jews it's offensive; to the Greeks, silliness

24 But to ALL who are called, whether Jew, whether Greek
   both God's Power and Wisdom are in Christ made Complete
25 Human wisdom is nothing next to God's foolishness
   human strength is impotent next to God's feebleness

26 Look around you, my brethren, very few V.I.P.'s
   very few rich and famous, very few royalty
27 God has chosen the foolish to perplex the profound
   God has chosen the feeble to bewilder the strong

28 God has chosen the low-down-common-run-of-the-mill-
   dime-a-dozen nobodies, to bring down the "who's who"
29 There's a very good reason He has done it this way
   God gets ALL of the Glory; we don't merit a thing

30 Our new thoughts; our new actions; our new start; our new Life
   these are gifts from our Father, through His Son Jesus Christ
31 It is written, God said it; "You've been blessed; celebrate!
   just remember Who did it; Yes, it's ALL about Me!"

        I Corinthians 1:18-31

They say the only way to You is through relationship
You leading me; You guiding me; You teaching me to live
a life that's pleasing in Your sight, according to Your will
me loving, praising, worshipping; me growing up in You

They tell me You are always near to lend a helping hand
if I'll just ask and seek and knock, You'll always let me in
You'll be a lamp unto my feet, a light unto my path
You'll lift me up; You'll give me strength, for each and every step

They tell me You will only help the ones who help themselves
They tell me I must do my best if I want You to help
They tell me to be diligent in studying the Word
They tell me I must act upon the truths that I have heard

They tell me always to consider, "What would Jesus do?"
They say this is the secret to becoming more like You
As I become more christ-like, You will come and live with me
a life of close communion, with no barriers between

They say our spirits must connect, but first I must obey
They tell me Jesus did His part; the rest is up to me
They tell me You will never bless a disobedient child
They tell me that I must confess, repent and change my style

This all sounds very well and good; it makes such common sense
there's only one small problem, and that problem is my flesh
The things I want to do, I don't; the things I don't, I do
it's not "what" will deliver me; no, it's not "what", but "Who!"

So shut me down and drag me out and nail me to the tree
just leave me there; don't cut me loose, until I'm history
Then fill me with Your Spirit; resurrect me in Your Light
Come live in me; without me; come be my Eternal Life!

                Romans 7

"And I, if I be lifted up from the earth, will draw ALL men unto me."
John 12:32

"For of Him, and through Him, and to Him, are ALL things: to whom be glory forever. Amen."
Romans 11:36

"And when ALL things shall be subdued unto Him, then shall the Son also Himself be subject unto Him that put ALL things under Him that God may be ALL in ALL."
I Corinthians 15:28

"Having made known unto us the mystery of His will, according to His good pleasure which He hath purposed in Himself: That in the dispensation of the fullness of times He might gather together in one ALL things in Christ, both which are in heaven, and which are on the earth, even in Him."
Ephesians 1:9, 10

"For by Him were ALL things created, that are in heaven, and that are in earth, visible and invisible, whether they be thrones, or dominions, or principalities, or powers: ALL things were created by Him, and for Him: And He is before ALL things, and by Him ALL things consist. And He is the head of the body, the church: who is the beginning, the firstborn from the dead; that in ALL things He might have the preeminence. For it pleased the Father that in Him should ALL fullness dwell. And, having made peace through the blood of His cross, by Him to reconcile ALL things unto Himself; by Him, I say, whether they be things in earth, or things in heaven."
Colossians 1:16-20

"For this is good and acceptable in the sight of God our Savior; who will have ALL men to be saved, and come to the knowledge of the truth. For there is one God, and one mediator between God and men, the man Jesus Christ; who gave Himself a ransom for ALL, to be testified in due time."

I Timothy 2:3-6

And He that sat upon the throne said, "Behold, I make ALL things new." And He said unto me, "Write; for these words are true and faithful."

Revelation 21:5

U. R.
~ INCLUDED ~
in "ALL" things!!!

Revelation 21:5

Thank *YOU, JESUS!!!*
it's *ALL (100%)* about YOU!!!

Amen.

*Jim (left) with co-worker Chuck Pates (right)
at Miller Park, Milwaukee, Wisconsin in 2001.*

Jim Muffo was born in 1955 to Paul and Evelyn Muffo in Menominee, Michigan. He graduated from Andrews Academy, Berrien Springs, Michigan in 1973. Jim is a 27-year union journeyman roofer living in South Bend, Indiana. He has been blessed with one son, one stepson, one granddaughter, and three grandsons.